SCIENCE WORLD

WEATHER

MARK PETTIGREW

Franklin Watts
London • Sydney

© Archon Press 2003

Produced by
Archon Press Ltd
28 Percy Street
London W1T 2BZ

New edition first published in
Great Britain in 2003 by
Franklin Watts
96 Leonard Street
London EC2A 4XD

Original edition published as
Simply Science – Weather

ISBN 0–7496–5106–7

Printed in UAE

All rights reserved

Editor: Harriet Brown

Designer: Flick, Book Design & Graphics

Picture Researcher: Brian Hunter Smart

Illustrator: Louise Nevett

A CIP record for this book is
available from the British Library.

CONTENTS

INTRODUCTION

An understanding of the weather is often vital to daily life – farmers, for example, require information about the weather to try and protect their crops. Extremes of weather can ruin entire crops.

Sometimes even our safety depends on knowing about weather conditions. With advance warning of a major storm, ships or aeroplanes can be routed away from danger. Flood warnings can be issued and people moved to a safe area.

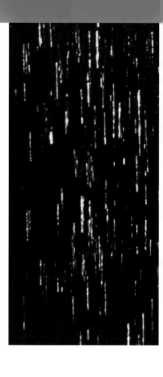

Farmers need to irrigate, or water, their crops if there is no rain.

In this book you will find out about the causes of weather, and you will see why different places are mainly hot or cold, wet or dry. You will discover why the weather changes through the year, and you will learn something about weather forecasting – how to predict the weather.

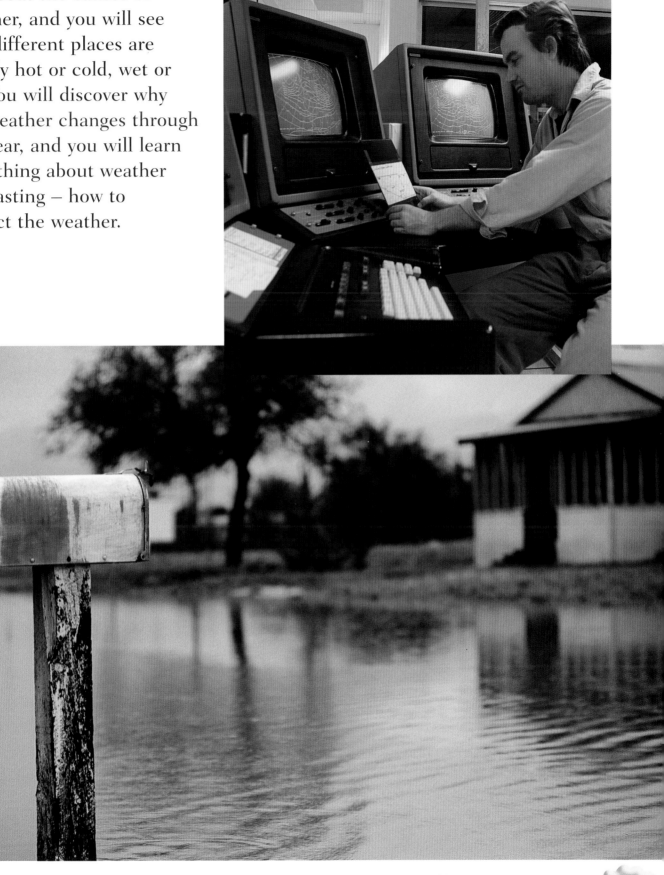

Heavy rain can cause rivers to burst their banks and flood large areas of land.

THE WEATHER

When we say "The Sun is shining", we are talking about the weather. However, when we say "It's always sunny here", we are talking about the climate. The climate describes the way weather behaves over many years. The climate depends on many factors, including how far from the equator a place is. Weather is caused by changes in the 'atmosphere' – the layer of air surrounding the Earth.

Generally, weather and climate are caused by parts of the world becoming warmer than others when the Sun's rays heat the Earth's surface. These differences in temperature make the air move and these air movements cause the different types of weather we know.

The changing weather – hot, sunny conditions in summer...

...heavy snow in winter. Some parts of the world get hurricanes – very strong winds (inset).

THE WIND

Winds carry warm and cold air around the world. Knowing which way the wind is blowing is a useful guide to the type of weather we can expect. Around the world, there are many differences in temperature. Air in contact with hot land or sea is warmed. As warm air is lighter than cooler air, it rises. Cooler air then moves in to take its place. This movement of air is what we call wind.

Winds can be extremely powerful; they can knock down trees, and can push along boats fitted with sails. The map on the opposite page shows the routes of the main winds across the globe. These routes were once followed by sailing ships carrying their cargoes around the world.

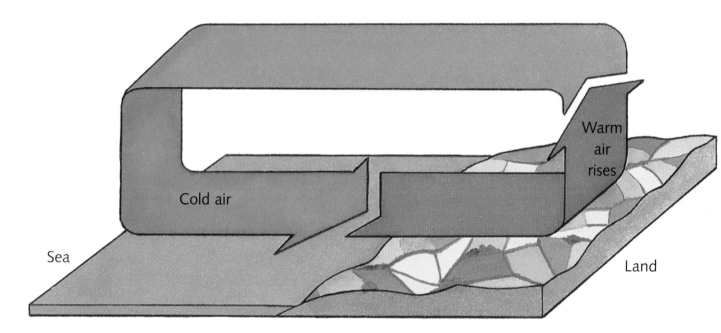

Warm air rises

Cold air

Sea

Land

Sea breezes

As the Sun shines, air over the land is heated more than air over the sea, and this hot air rises. Cooler air from over the sea moves in to take its place.

The hot air cools as it rises, but it does not fall straight back down. Instead, it spreads out over the sea and falls down there. This circular air current causes an onshore breeze.

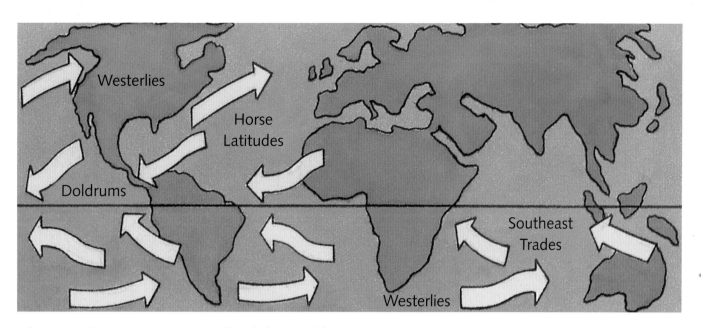

Westerlies

Horse
Latitudes

Doldrums

Southeast
Trades

Westerlies

The map shows the major winds of the world.

Yachts with the wind in their sails

CLOUDS

Clouds are formed from water vapour. The air collects this vapour as it passes over damp places, like the sea. We call the process of a liquid turning to a gas 'evaporation'. Normally, the vapour in the air is invisible, but if the air is cooled then clouds of tiny water droplets are formed. This process we call 'condensation'.

The amount of water vapour that the air can carry depends on how hot the air is – warmer air can carry more moisture. When warm, moist air rises, either by moving over hills and mountains, or by meeting cooler air, it is cooled. As the air cools, it can carry less vapour. The excess moisture forms clouds of tiny droplets.

Storm clouds gathering

The fluffy, white clouds you see on fine, summer days are called 'cumulus'.

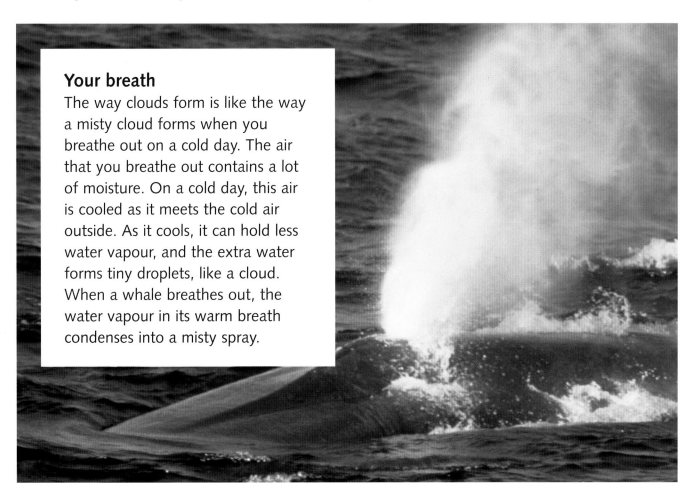

Your breath

The way clouds form is like the way a misty cloud forms when you breathe out on a cold day. The air that you breathe out contains a lot of moisture. On a cold day, this air is cooled as it meets the cold air outside. As it cools, it can hold less water vapour, and the extra water forms tiny droplets, like a cloud. When a whale breathes out, the water vapour in its warm breath condenses into a misty spray.

RAIN AND SNOW

The tiny water droplets inside a cloud may bump into each other and join together to form larger droplets. If the air inside a cloud is rising, these droplets are lifted up again and join with others to form yet larger droplets. When the droplets are very large, about the size of raindrops, the rising air can no longer lift the drops back up and so they fall as rain.

The water cycle

This diagram shows how the evaporation of water caused by sunshine makes the air moist. Moist air travelling inland may have to rise over hills and this cools it. As the rising air is cooled, clouds form and rain may fall. The rain falling on the land runs into streams, which flow into rivers. The river water eventually returns to the sea.

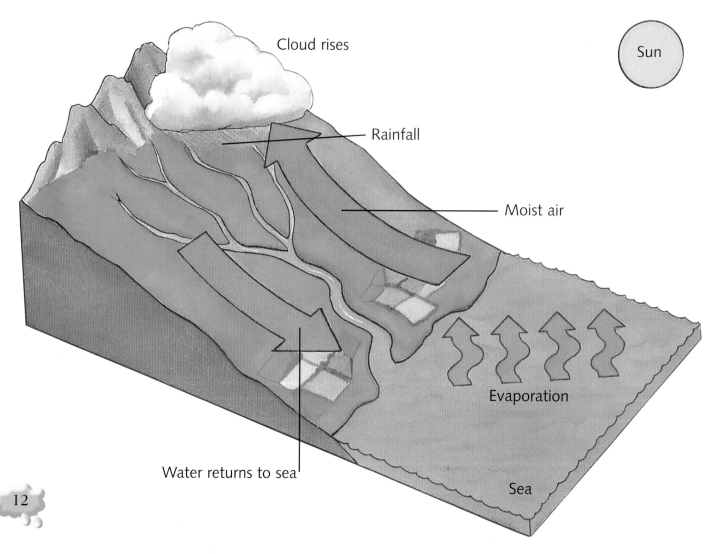

Cloud rises

Sun

Rainfall

Moist air

Evaporation

Water returns to sea

Sea

Seen under a microscope, snowflakes have intricate patterns.

If the air inside a cloud is very cold, snowflakes may be formed. A snowflake is formed by water vapour below freezing point condensing upon dust in the clouds. Tiny drops of water may hit the snowflakes in the cloud and freeze to ice, making the snowflakes larger.

If there is a strong current of air upwards inside a cloud, the falling pieces of ice may be lifted back up, and more ice will form on the outside. This process is repeated until, eventually, the ice is so heavy it falls to the ground as hail.

Hail can form very large balls of ice.

13

AIR PRESSURE

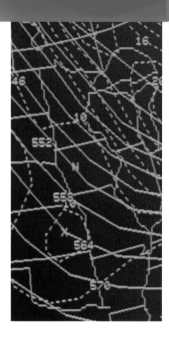

We usually think of air as being weightless, but in fact air is quite heavy. The air in a large classroom has the same weight as a small car! The air of the Earth's atmosphere reaches upwards for several hundred kilometres. The effect of this is that the air at ground level presses on everything it surrounds.

The exact air pressure changes from day to day. Studying air pressure, and the way it is changing, helps to tell us how the weather will change in the next few hours and days. Usually, high pressure brings good weather whereas low pressure brings bad weather. A device called a 'barometer' measures air pressure and is used to predict the weather.

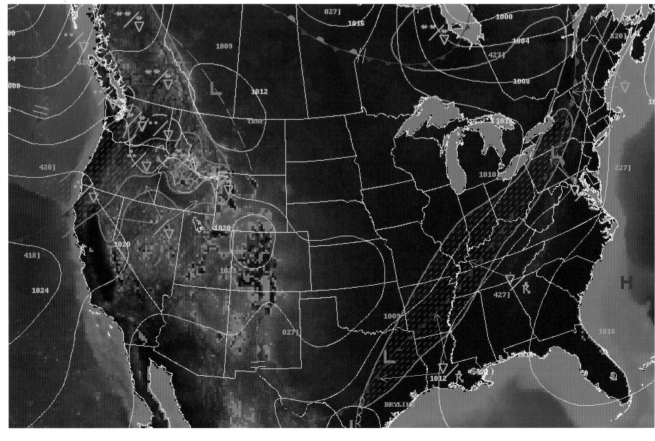

On this map you can see areas of high pressure (H) and low pressure (L).

The effects of air pressure

You can see an effect of air pressure with a washing-up liquid bottle. If you remove most of the air from inside the bottle, by sucking it, the bottle collapses. This is because the air around it pushes inwards. Normally the air inside balances this force. Simple barometers measure changes in pressure in a similar way.

Large swirls of cloud like this one often indicate areas of low air pressure.

WEATHER ON THE MOVE

Weather forecasting is partly done by looking at the movements of 'fronts' – regions where warm air meets cooler air. The warm air at a front rises over the cooler air. This cools the warm air and so rain often falls near fronts.

Where warm and cool air meet, the warm air may become partly surrounded by cooler air. As warm air causes lower pressure, this creates a low pressure area called a 'depression'. When a depression moves over us, we can expect unsettled, rainy or stormy weather.

A high pressure region called an 'anticyclone' forms where cool air is surrounded by warmer air. An anticyclone moves slowly and can mean a long period of dry or sunny weather.

 16   Bad weather can make driving very dangerous.

Movement of fronts

The region where cold air pushes against a mass of warm air is called a 'cold front'.

The cold air burrows under the warm air (1) causing it to rise, and so clouds and rain are formed in the rising air.

The cold front catches up with a warm front, where warm air moves into a region of colder air (2). Here, the warm air rises over the cold air, causing more clouds and rain.

Eventually the cold air on the left catches up with the cold air on the right, and the warm air is lifted above ground level (3).

Finally, the warm air disappears, and we just see a region of cool air moving over a region of colder air (4).

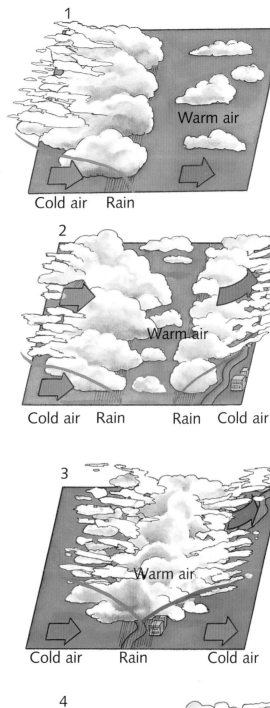

1

Warm air

Cold air   Rain

2

Warm air

Cold air   Rain   Rain   Cold air

3

Warm air

Cold air   Rain   Cold air

Key

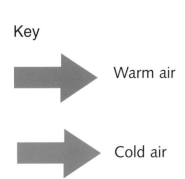

Warm air

Cold air

4

Cold air warms up   Rain   Cold air

17

STORMY WEATHER

Sometimes the weather can be extremely violent. One of the most severe types of weather is a hurricane, which may happen near tropical oceans.

Another violent form of weather is a thunderstorm. Thunderstorms happen in extremely moist air, where the grey-black thundercloud stretches up several thousand metres. Inside a thundercloud there are fast air currents which cause 'static electricity', electric charge, to build up inside the cloud. Lightning and thunder occur when this electric charge leaps from cloud to cloud or to the ground. The fast air currents inside thunderclouds can hold up large raindrops and so produce very heavy rain.

Thunderstorms can cause bolts of lightning to jump from a cloud to the ground.

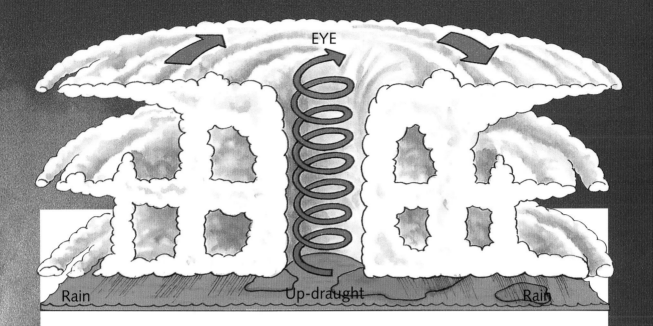

EYE

Rain   Up-draught   Rain

Inside a hurricane

In the centre of a hurricane, called the 'eye', there is very little wind. Around the eye, there are very strong winds spiralling round and upwards. Further out there are swirling regions of cloud, reaching perhaps 50 km across. These clouds produce torrential rain.

A thunderstorm over
the sea – an example
of the weather's power

LOOKING AT THE CLIMATE

The most important factor that influences the climate of a place is its distance from the equator – the imaginary line around the centre of the Earth. Places further away from the equator are usually cooler than places that are nearer. This is because the Sun's light is spread over a larger area towards the Earth's poles and it has to travel through more of the atmosphere to get there.

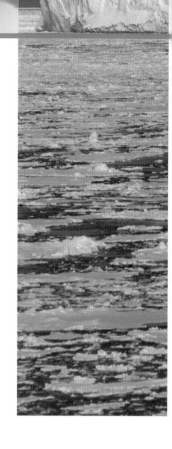

Climate and the sea

Places far from the sea, or hidden from the sea by great mountain ranges, often have very little rainfall – the air reaching them has already lost most of its moisture as rain on its journey over the land.

Places near to the sea do not usually have great temperature changes. The sea heats up much more slowly than the land and cools more slowly. Therefore, it keeps the land warm in winter and cool in summer.

Deserts often have little rainfall because they are sheltered by mountain ranges.

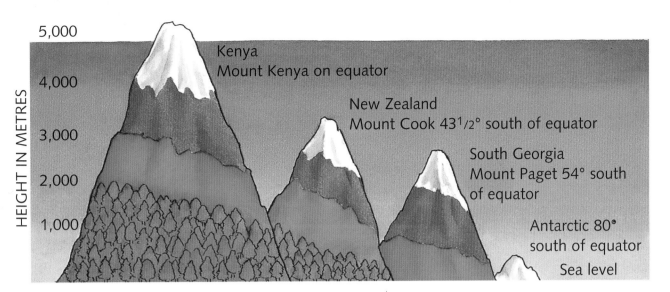

HEIGHT IN METRES

5,000
4,000
3,000
2,000
1,000

Kenya
Mount Kenya on equator

New Zealand
Mount Cook 43¹/₂° south of equator

South Georgia
Mount Paget 54° south
of equator

Antarctic 80°
south of equator
Sea level

The climate is affected by how high up you are and where in the world you are. As you go higher, the climate becomes cooler and eventually too cold for trees to grow. Even higher, the ground is covered by snow all year round. The 'snow line' and 'tree line' become lower as you move away from the equator.

Here you can see the snow line and the tree line on the side of the mountain.

21

THE SEASONS

As the Earth spins on its axis, it orbits about the Sun. This means that at different times of year, different parts of the world directly face the Sun in the middle of the day. In January, places about 2,000 kilometres south of the equator have the hottest weather. In July, the hottest weather is about 2,000 kilometres north of the equator. This means that the warmest season in the northern parts of the world is during July and in the southern part during January.

Many climates further away from the equator have four seasons. The weather in winter is often too cold for most plants to grow, and there is a good deal of frost. In summer and winter the weather is often stable for longer periods of time. The weather in spring and autumn often changes from day to day, with high winds and sudden showers. The main season of growth is spring.

Winter   Spring   Summer   Autumn

As the hottest regions change, the directions of winds and positions of fronts change around the world. These winds and fronts affect rainfall, and so some regions have distinct rainy and dry seasons. In India, for example, there is a very rainy summer season, called the wet 'monsoon', but little or no rain from December to April.

The wet monsoon often causes flooding.

RECORDING WEATHER

Around the world, weather stations record the type of weather every day – they monitor the temperature continuously, the amount of rainfall and the hours of sunshine. Air pressure, which affects the weather, is also recorded. Measuring the 'humidity', or amount of moisture in the air, helps to predict clouds, fog or rain.

Satellites can be used in long-range weather forecasting – predicting the weather for a period of weeks. They orbit the Earth photographing it and recording weather patterns. Information sent back to the Earth could include warnings of a fast-developing storm in the tropics, or of a sudden snow melt in a mountainous region.

Recording sunshine

A sunshine recorder uses a large round lens to focus the Sun's rays and burn a mark onto a piece of card. As the Sun moves across the sky, the burn mark leaves a trail showing how long the Sun has been shining.

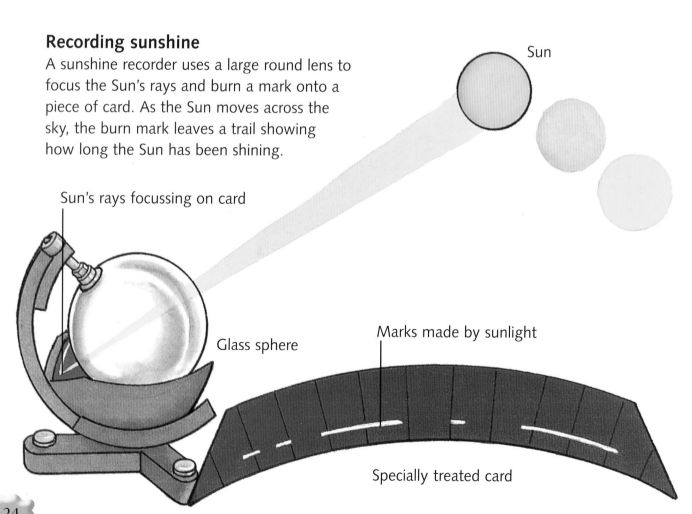

Sun

Sun's rays focussing on card

Glass sphere

Marks made by sunlight

Specially treated card

The weather satellite Tiros orbits the Earth recording the weather.

WEATHER FORECASTS

Most people like to know in advance what the weather will be like. Weather forecasters often look for signs of fronts approaching – as a warm front approaches, the air pressure decreases and as a cold front approaches the air pressure increases. These *changes* in pressure often bring rain. A *steady* area of high pressure often says we can expect dry weather, cold in winter, warm in summer. Professional weather forecasters may use radar to watch how the clouds are moving. Information can also be processed by a computer to show, for example, temperature differences.

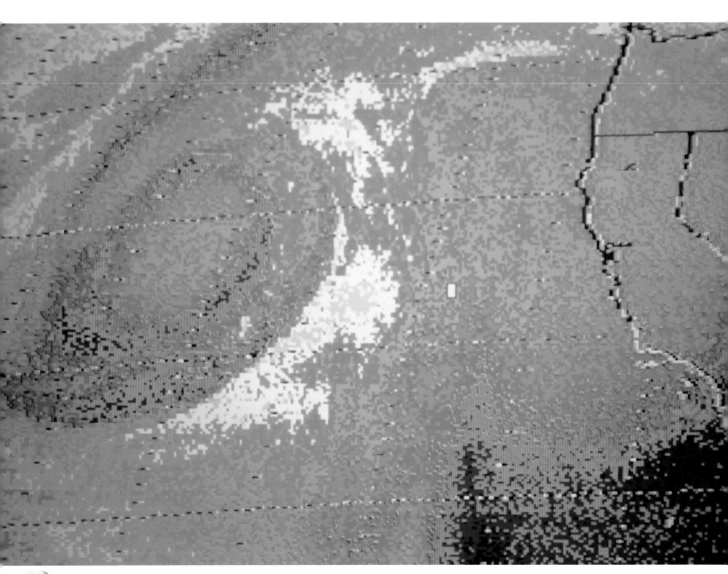

Satellite images can show a storm developing.

Many well-known sayings help amateur weather forecasters to predict the weather. "Red sky at night, shepherds' delight", says that a red sunset will bring dry and warm weather.

Pine cones are also a tool for the amateur weather forecaster. When the air is moist, just before rainfall, pine cones close their scales. In dry weather, the scales open again.

Red sky at night – good weather the next day?

MAKE YOUR OWN WEATHER BASE

Weather forecasters record many observations to predict the weather. By making this weather base you can also record the weather. Make the scales on each instrument by comparing your readings with those given in the weather forecast.

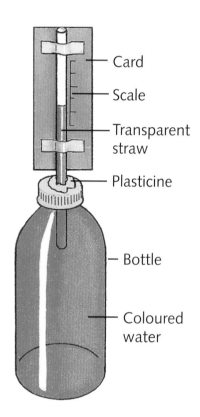

- Card
- Scale
- Transparent straw
- Plasticine
- Bottle
- Coloured water

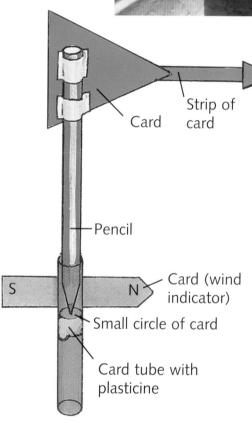

- Strip of card
- Card
- Pencil
- Card (wind indicator)
- Small circle of card
- S
- N
- Card tube with plasticine

Thermometer

You need a glass bottle with a screw top. Ask a grown-up to make a hole in the top. Fill the bottle with water coloured with food colouring. Push a straw through the hole. Cut out a card scale and attach it to the straw with tape. Make sure the water goes up into the straw – add drops through the straw if necessary.

Wind vane

Fit a card tube around a pencil. Cut two triangles and a strip of card to make a vane. Attach them together as shown and then attach the vane to the pencil with tape. Cut the wind indicator as shown. Rest the point of the pencil on the small circle held in place by plasticine inside the tube. Use a compass to mark north and south on the wind indicator.

Weather base

Use sturdy card to make a box big enough to hold the different instruments. Paint the box with household paint to help protect it. Make a door for the 'weather base' by cutting out another piece of card to size. Cut six slits in the door of the box to allow the air to circulate freely. Now attach it to the box with sticky-tape hinges.

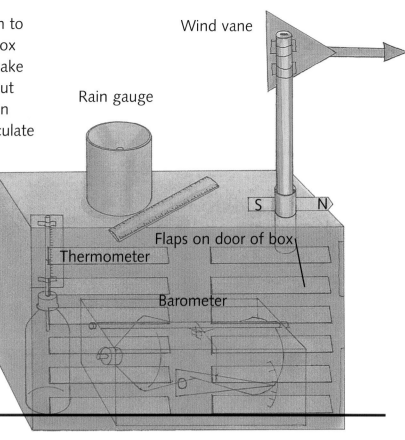

Wind vane

Rain gauge

S   N

Flaps on door of box

Thermometer

Barometer

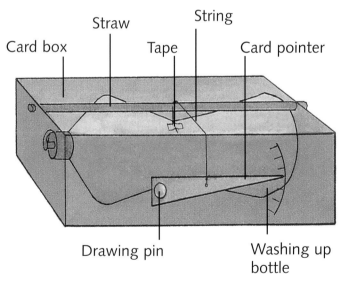

Card box
Straw
String
Tape
Card pointer

Drawing pin
Washing up bottle

Barometer

Squeeze out air from a washing-up liquid bottle. Replace the top. Slot a straw through a box as shown. Loop a piece of string over the straw. Attach one end to the bottle, and the other to a pointer fastened to the box with a drawing pin. The pointer moves up as the air pressure increases and down as it decreases.

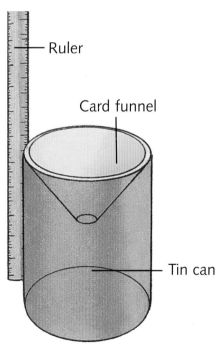

Ruler

Card funnel

Tin can

Rain gauge

Measure the diameter of a tin. Cut a card triangle so the longest side is the same size as the tin's diameter. Tape the two short edges of the triangle together to make a funnel. Put it in the tin. Use a ruler to measure the rainfall.

MORE ABOUT CLOUDS

The fluffy, white clouds you see on fine, summer days are called 'cumulus' clouds. When these rise up to form dark 'cumulo-nimbus' thunderclouds, there is a good chance of a heavy shower or a thunderstorm.

'Cirrus' clouds are the thin, wispy clouds you sometimes see very high in the sky on dry days. They usually mean a front is arriving, so you can expect the weather to change. As a front moves nearer, the cloud gets lower, turning into 'alto-stratus' or small 'alto-cumulus'. Tall heaps of alto-cumulus mean there may be a storm. Lower down, grey 'nimbo-stratus' clouds often cause continuous rain. 'Stratus' clouds form as a low sheet and often cause fog.

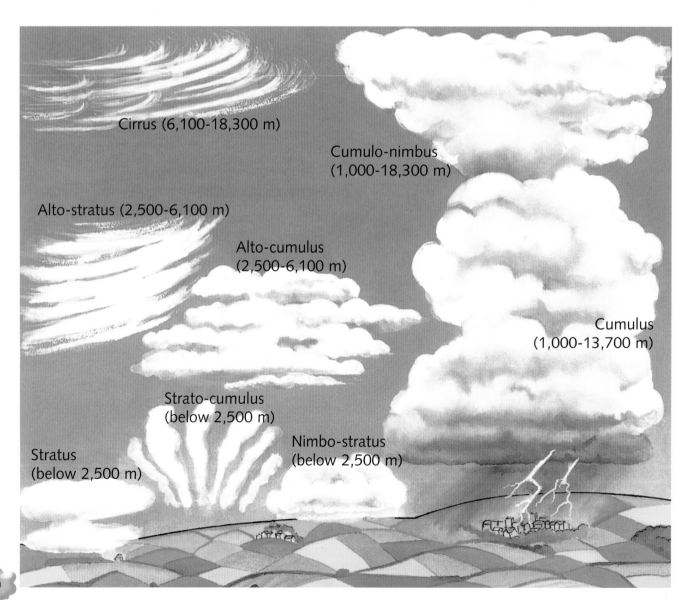

Cirrus (6,100-18,300 m)

Cumulo-nimbus
(1,000-18,300 m)

Alto-stratus (2,500-6,100 m)

Alto-cumulus
(2,500-6,100 m)

Cumulus
(1,000-13,700 m)

Strato-cumulus
(below 2,500 m)

Nimbo-stratus
(below 2,500 m)

Stratus
(below 2,500 m)

GLOSSARY

Air pressure
The air of the atmosphere presses against everything it surrounds. The effect of this is called the air pressure.

Anticyclone
An area of high pressure. Winds spiral round and away from an anticyclone. An anticyclone can bring a prolonged period of dry or sunny weather.

Atmosphere
The layer of air surrounding the Earth.

Barometer
A device used to measure changes in air pressure. These are used to help predict the weather.

Climate
The pattern of weather conditions which exists in a place over a period of many years.

Condensation
As water vapour turns to a liquid it condenses. You can see condensation happening by breathing onto a cold window pane.

Depression
An area of low pressure. Depressions usually bring unsettled, stormy weather.

Equator
The imaginary line around the middle of the Earth.

Evaporation
The opposite of condensation – when a liquid changes into a gas, without boiling.

Front
The region where masses of cold and warm air push against each other. Fronts often bring rain.

Hail
Large pieces of ice which fall to the ground from very cold thunderclouds.

Snow
Snow is caused by the condensation of water vapour in particles of dust in the clouds at temperatures below freezing point. Each snowflake has its own shape – when seen under a microscope they appear as an endless variety of six-sided crystals.

Snow line
An imaginary line drawn to show the height above which the land is covered by snow all year round. The height of the snow line is affected by the distance from the equator.

Static electricity
Electric charge that can form in thunderclouds and cause lightning.

Tree line
An imaginary line above which it is too cold for trees to grow. Both the snow line and the tree line become lower further away from the equator.

Water vapour
When water evaporates it forms a gas – water vapour. Water vapour is found in the atmosphere.

Weather
The conditions of the atmosphere at any particular moment.

Wind
The movement of air from one place to another. This movement causes our varying weather conditions from day to day.

INDEX

Photocredits

Abbreviations: l-left, r-right, b-bottom, t-top, c-centre, m-middle

Front cover main, back cover main, front cover mt, 1, 2-3, 4tl, 4tr, 5 both, 6tl, 6tr, 7 both, 8tl, 8tr, 10 all, 11t, 12tl, 14tl, 14tr, 16 all, 17, 18 all, 19, 20tl, 20tr, 22tl, 24tl, 26tl, 26b, 27b, 28tl, 30t, 31t, 32t — Corbis. Front cover mb, 12tr, 22bl, 28tr — Select Pictures. 4b — USDA. 6b — Argentinian Embassy, London. 9b, 11b — Corel. 13t — Bruce Coleman. 13b, 14b — NOAA Photo Library. 15, 24tr — NASA. 20b, 21b, 22tr, 26tr — Digital Stock. 23 — Robert Harding. 25 — Zefa. 27tr — US National Park Service. 29ml — Roger Vlitos.